Library of Congress Cataloging-in-Publication Data:

Mighty Fine.
Oui, oui Waikiki : featuring French Kitty / by Mighty Fine.
p. cm.
Includes bibliographical references and index.
ISBN 0-8109-4816-8
1. Cats—Poetry. 2. Hawaii—Poetry. I. Title.

PS3613.I37O94 2004
811'.6—dc22
2003020926

Original illustrations and design by Mighty Fine™

www.french-kitty.com

Published in 2004 by Harry N. Abrams, Incorporated, New York.

Printed and bound in China
10 9 8 7 6 5 4 3 2 1

Harry N. Abrams, Inc.
100 Fifth Avenue
New York, NY 10011

Oui, Oui, Waikiki

Featuring French Kitty® by Mighty Fine™

Harry N. Abrams, Inc., Publishers

for Kai

The icy-cold weather
had lasted so long,
Kitty was wishing
for dances and song.

fifi la foo

miss kitty kat
& birdie too
nyc, usa

As she thought to herself,
I *need* a vacation
Birdie flew in
with a pink invitation.

Your presence is crucial,
my darling sweet puss!
Come meet my love Rolf.
He is JUST <u>fab-u-luss</u>!

Love, Fifi

P.S. Bring
Birdie too!

Please come
to our
Hawaiian luau
by the sea.

We'll be married
tomorrow in
warm Waikiki!

"Tomorrow? He's crazy!

We've no time to delay!
We need sunscreen, sunglasses ...
There's simply no way!"

"Birdie, calm down.
We'll make our flight.
Fifi also sent tickets ...

...we leave late tonight!"

Waikiki, Oahu,
Hawai'i fan-tropical!
On landing they dreamed
flora-exotical!

"Aloha kakahiaka"

"The Kakawiwilaniwanapipi Hotel
is spectacular!" Birdie exclaimed
in Hawaiian vernacular.

"Aloha," snorted the clerk,
who checked their reservation,
as Kitty was struck with
a cruel realization.

"No pilik

MR. SW

"We remembered our sunscreen
and sunglasses, too ...
but we've forgotten a present
for Fifi La Foo!"

"Don't worry," cooed the clerk, who had been eavesdropping. "This island has simply stupendous gift shopping."

"Right next door's just the thing
to bring newlyweds luck ..."

QUEEN BIKI'S BOU- TIQUE

"Wiki wiki"

WORLD'S
LARGEST
TIKI
HUT

"Kokua!"

Inside the boutique,
they found tikis galore ...

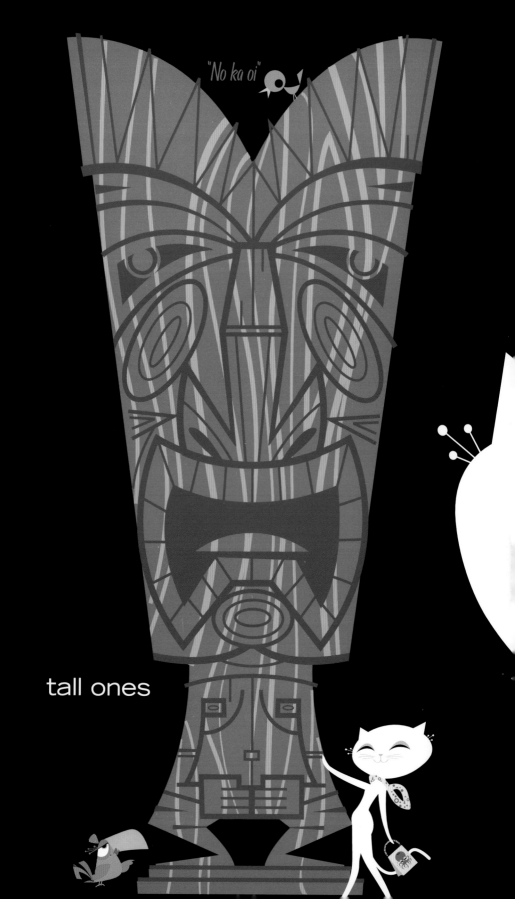

"No ka oi"

tall ones

and squat ones

and
wee
ones
and
more!

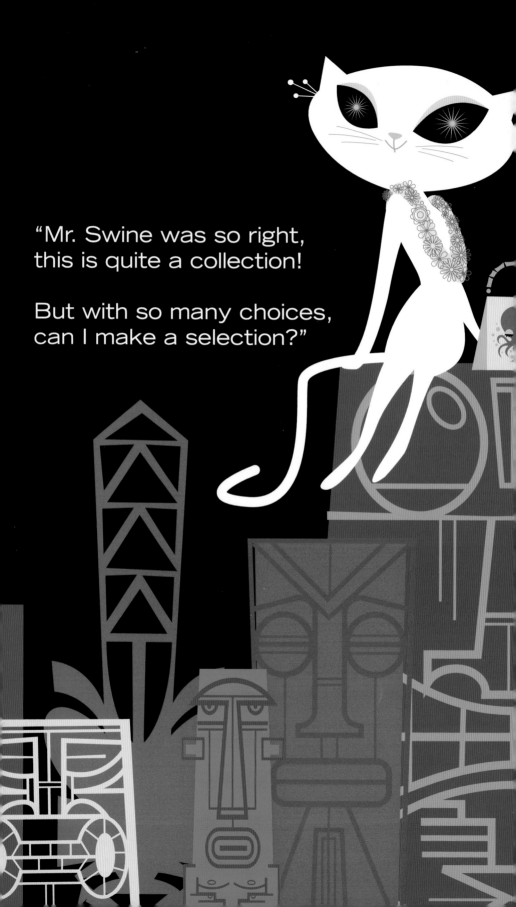

"Mr. Swine was so right,
this is quite a collection!

But with so many choices,
can I make a selection?"

This wasn't the first time Queen Biki had heard this.

She knowingly offered, "Can I be of service?"

"Hele"

Just then, with a twang of his ukulele guitar, entered Prince Hunka Hunka, local boy island star!

"Aloha Oi, Queenie! Catch my lounge act tonight?"

While the Queen explained
the pair's frustration

"A hui hou"

Kitty was struck by true inspiration!

Later that night
at Rolf and Fifi's soireé
the food was delicious,
the mood enchanté.

Rolf said, "Fabelhaft, darling!
The floor show's divine.
Why, the performer looks
alarmingly like our Mr. Swine."

"Ladies and gents, may
I introduce the next act—"
"Wait a minute," said Fifi,
"where's my friend Kitty Kat?"

"Quiet please!"
oinked the boar.
"I need your attention!
This next act's performed
by the kitten just mentioned!"

Soon to be followed
by Prince Hunka too.
As her present to Fifi
on this special day,
she would sing a sweet song
sung simply this way ...

"Love is a thing
you can't sell or buy.
I'm glad that you've found
such a wonderful guy."

"Hana hou!"

The sweet song
inspired a standing ovation ...

...and it was only the first day of Kitty's vacation!

Aloha!

Hawaiian Glossary

Aloha kakahiaka—Good morning

No pilikia—Don't worry

Wiki wiki—Hurry up

Kokua—Help

No ka oi—The best

Hele—Let's go

Ono-licious—Delicious

A hui hou—Until we meet again

Hana hou—Encore

Shakas—Excellent

Pau—End

And Maika'i no means

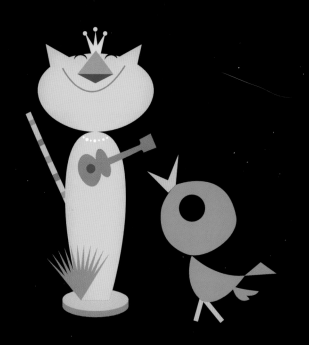

Everything's Fine!